This book is dedicated to Bishop Darrell Harmon and Pastor Sheryl Harmon for you all kindness and devotion and endless support of God's House Of Worship family. I admire your sense of humor. Respect your love for God. Adore your character. Love the way you nurture your family, sisters, and brothers. A fly grandfather and grandmother. Awesome friend. Loyal general in the Lord's army. Great sister and brother in law. All these words are you both.

The Suit

THE BATTLES INSIDE OUR MARRIAGE

Tonia M Phillips

authorHOUSE®

AuthorHouse™
1663 Liberty Drive
Bloomington, IN 47403
www.authorhouse.com
Phone: 1 (800) 839-8640

Published by AuthorHouse   04/21/2016

ISBN: 978-1-5246-0488-2 (sc)
ISBN: 978-1-5246-0487-5 (e)

Library of Congress Control Number: 2016906567

Print information available on the last page.

Contents

Marriage is a sacred vow between a man and woman. First of all let me say this.

The good book the Bible says this about marriage "what God has joined together let no man put asunder." Now you asked yourself the most important question that one can ask. Is my marriage born of God or man? We find ourselves later in life asking this question, "Lord was it you or me that joined myself together as one?" Marriage plays a great part in our lives. I watch just about all my children commit themselves to other people. Even I, with just about twenty years, now come to understand the difference in what God joins and not what we as men and women do to each other. When I was young, in my early years, I wanted to believe in Cinderella because I was shown the movie of a knight riding on a horse to take me away and we would live in a palace. But little did I know that was not for me, a little African American girl with a dream of marriage. I found out later in life that if you do not seek God for the right answers then the answers that come with marriage will take forever to be revealed. Possibilities come with conditions. The only handbook that was given to us in the directions of marriage is the Word of God. Marriage by God's design is the union of a male and female and not male and male or female and female. When God joins male and female together we become as one flesh and one body, not two people. The word says "therefore a man leaves his mother and father and cleave unto his wife making them become one flesh."**(Genesis 2:24)** On the day of my marriage to my husband, little did he know that was the first wedding dress I had ever worn. After two failed marriages, one a contract, and the other happened when I left my parents home at the age of eighteen and ran off and got married. You may say I was old enough to get married, but the mind I had at this time was to leave a home that brought me happiness and sadness. Because of this, my wedding on March 13,1996 was to me a real marriage with cake, flowers, songs and the dressed up family. Oh don't let me leave out my knight in white armor!

Chapter One
When a man finds a woman

Proverbs 18:22

"Whosoever findeth a wife he findeth a good thing, and obtaineth favor of the lord." I did not know of this verse when I was younger, no one in the church that I grew up in spoke on these things, how God's favor came to him for finding a good wife. Not just any woman but a woman of God's own heart. Every man has a rib that comes from the creation of his side just like Adam and Eve. Ephesians 5:33 "Nevertheless let every one of you in particular so love his wife even as himself and the wife see that she reverence her husband." The word reverence is not one that I had ever used to honor my husband. I felt a respect for him as he respected me. If he did not respect my feelings then I would not respect his. I only wanted to give to him as much as he had given to me, no more and very less of me. The power of hurt was still on my plate.I had not forgiven and closed the other chapter of my two failed marriages.

Ephesians 5:25 "Husbands, love your wives, even as Christ also love the church, and gave himself for it." I loved my new husband and still do today, but the lesson I had to learn was that love comes with a high cost and will I continue to fail at marriage or fight for my marriage?

Ephesians 5:22-33 "wives, submit yourselves unto your own husbands, as unto the Lord." Now this passage gets us all into trouble. You say how can I submit unto a man that is not following the Lord? What I have learned in the years of my marriage is that I must follow the Lord and obey His word. He will do the cleaning up of my husband. I spent so many years trying to clean him up myself, not depending on the work of God's power. I was running on my own power and making more of a mess than I was willing to take. I believed it was my way or no way. Finally it hit me that I was not in control of my marriage, the almighty God was, if I let Him. Finally I realized that I was doing more harm than good, so I had to let go of the dream about the knight in the shining armor to take back my marriage. My knight did not come to me riding on a black horse with a gold shield or golden breastplate.

He came to me in a dream one night when the Lord showed me a man giving me a new watch. In the dream we were in love with each other, a love that felt like real love. Now you ask me what real love feels like? You know, the kind of love that when you grow old and your hair falls out, your husband says to you "honey look how long your hair is and you are still beautiful to me...that does not matter to me, I still love you." That's the real love that another human can give to you. There is a special kind of love that only comes from God and His son Jesus. This love covers a multitude of sins. And His love teaches us how to love one another in our marriage.

Chapter Two
Subject ye one to another

Proverbs 12:4 "A wife of noble character is her husband's crown, but a disgraceful wife is like decay in his bones."

Sometimes we forget that honor is precious to the Lord when we take our place as a wife. This became a part of my learning some years ago. I had to learn to stop wanting control and to honor my husband as being the head of my house. In some cases, his actions did not please me and I would shout out words of angry and disgust, only because he would not listen to my solutions but acted on his. I again believed it to be my way or the highway. Boy was I wrong! There is a scripture that says "houses and wealth are inherited from parents, **but a prudent** (acting with or showing care and thought for the future). **wife is from the Lord.**" With much care I have come to the understanding that in all things give the Lord thanks even in the bad times too.

Chapter Three
May your fountain be blessed

◆————————————◆

In the middle of a struggling marriage, it's very easy to focus on what's wrong instead of what's right. In about ten years of my marriage, I had not stopped to listen to the Lord and things kept coming my way. Guidance was not an option with me at this time. I could not believe that here we were ten years into this marriage and it was still the same old thing. His wanting to have his pie and cake too. Me, in the leadership role as the head. Kinda like a bobtail bossy woman mentality. We both were out of place in our relationship and we both needed guidance to reclaim our rightful positions again. Men trying to change their wives and wives trying to change their husbands just won't work. You have to give it to God and that's when the change begins.

Proverbs 5:18-19.

"May your fountain be blessed and may you rejoice in the wife of your youth. As a loving deer and a graceful deer-may her breasts satisfy you always, may you ever be captivated by her love." Love on each other as much as you can. We never know when death do us part or sickness or bad health may pass our way. These are words highly spoken in your vows while facing each other and ringing of commitment in God's ears and loved ones looking on your special day.

Chapter Four

Faithfulness

Proverbs 20:6-7. "Many a man claims to have unfailing love, but a faithful man who can find? The righteous man leads a blameless life; blessed are his children after him." I remember my daughter talking to me about how she ran into one of her childhood friends and they asked her how is your mother and father? She said they are good. The question was are they still together? Because when you see your daddy you see your mother also, they are always together. When I heard this complement it surprised me to know that someone was watching. When two people that share the same kind of love enjoy each other, it shows. I remember when my mother told my daddy she loved him as he was headed out to work, he turned around and said you are suppose to love me like the Bible says. That was a test for my mother, the sign of hurt that brushed her face as he left the room she replied "I will never tell you that again" and she did not. The communication between my parents was bittersweet growing up. My father, the hard pill to swallow and my mother the cotton candy of the family. I watched so much growing up in our household. Cotton candy trying to keep us in love and respect for each other while dealing with no one ever loved me. She had given birth to fourteen kids just for love, because

there was so much unkindness with her childhood.

The hard pill to swallow was a man of God. He loved

on the lord with a hardness that I found out later

was a leak of love too. He believe in saving one soul

from the pits of hell, but he don't practice the other

part of the Bible that a man should love his wife as

himself and love his children as God loves children.

The men in her life (two) husbands, one unfaithful;

the other too religious to help her. Cotton candy

had given her life to the welfare of our family. She

would mention that if we did not stay together the

devil would pick us off one by one. These remarks

have stayed with me all of my life. If we don't hang in

here as husbands and wives, the devil can pick us off

one by one. A house divided can't stand...just like my

parent's relationship, it did not stand. I believe in my

heart that my parents forgave each other after their separation. My cotton candy passed away first, but not before asking forgiveness from her husband and children. My hard pill to swallow went some three years later. His passing hit me the hardest because I never got the chance to ask him, "how did you not know how much I loved you?" When I asked him for his last name he never gave me a answer.

Chapter Five

War and battles

―――◆―――✦―――◆―――

Deuteronomy 24:5 "if a man has recently married, he must not be sent to war or have any duty laid on him. For one year he is to be free to stay at home and bring happiness to the wife he has married." I remember my full year, how everything we did was wonderful and full of love. One time my husband made a statement to me "I love you so much that

I would give my life for you." Boy did I believe he was deeply in love with me! It would make my heart rejoice to hear those words. Then later as the months and years passed, we fall on hard times. Every marriage has it testing moments. When you feel like your partner does not understand you anymore, this makes the problems harder and heavier to bare. You feel a sense of loneliness creeping into your marriage and further down into the dark places in your mind. We are not communication with each other; no holding of hands, kissing, caressing, or passion and much to your surprise he turns his back and says "I don't want to talk about it." All your hopes of love have gone out the window and you tell yourself "I have made a big mistake marrying this crazy man, what was I thinking? But it never comes to your mind to rebuke satan because it's his thoughts and words that play over and over in your head like a scene from a movie or a script from the last novel you read. You find yourself playing the past over and over in your mind, remembering how we use to be. God asks us to lay our gifts at the altar and get it right with our brothers and sisters...this means spouses as well. We cannot go on fighting with each other and hoping for a blessed marriage, it won't happen. The keys to both of our hearts was prayer and forgiveness.

Chapter Six
Marital Duty

I Corinthians 7:1-10. "Now for the matters you wrote about: it is good for a man not to marry. But since there is so much immorality, each man should have his own wife, and each woman her own husband. The wife's body does not belong to her alone but to her husband. In the same way, the husband's body does not belong to him alone but also to his wife. Do not deprive each other except by mutual consent and for a time, so that you may devote yourself to prayer. Then come together again so that satan will not tempt you because of your lack of self control." The world tries to tell us that it's ok to have a lover or two. But God says no! That's not the way. When we look at the television and most of the time, maybe all of the time, our movies today are about lust. Who is sleeping with whom or how many lovers I can have. When I was little it was a disgrace to even talk about what a man and his wife did in the bedroom. Now these days, our children can tell you of conversations that are taking place with their classmates. Loving emotions between a husband and wife are precious, we don't act unseemly or improper or engaged with each other in worldly pleasures, meaning don't lust but love.

The righteousness of God's word will always stand no matter what, who, why and how.

Chapter Seven
Wisdom

There are two types of wisdom man wisdom and Godly wisdom. In our relationships, we have to know the difference. Man thinks from the brain, but God speaks to the heart. Marriage is a bond between what is holy and unholy. What is right and what is wrong. Let me explain; the holiness in our marriage is to put the Lord first, the unholy is to walk through your marriage without the Lord believing you are in control of every situation. God has said, 'Never will I leave you; never will I forsake you." So we say with confidence "the Lord is my helper, I will not be afraid.

Chapter Eight
Friendship with Each Other

———————◆———✳———◆———————

Ecclesiastes 4:9-10

"Two are better than one, because they have a good return for their work. If one falls down, his friend can help him up. But pity the man who falls and has no one to help him up!" We see that two heads are always better than one. The art to marriage is love and discipline, working together in order to become a canvas of love. The painter takes his time in painting a portrait. He looks at every stroke of his brush on the paper, imaging what it will look like when it's finished. That's what our marriage is like, working to see perfection. Understanding one another can bring out the best in ways that simplify our behavior. Learning to get along and compromising with each other's thoughts and feelings will better the relationship. Just try it!

Chapter Nine

The Wedding Retreat

———————✦———✦———✦———————

Isaiah 1:17 "Stop doing wrong, learn to do right!"

This weekend I went to our Church's (God's House of Worship) first marriage retreat. The speakers Bishop and Pastor Thomas from Beaumont, Texas were our speakers. As I sat in class my heart was open to receive instructions to bring more understanding into my marriage. Proverbs 12:18 "reckless words pierce like a sword, but the tongue of the wise brings healing." We must always watch the words that we speak. Walking in my marriage became hard. I had an understanding of how powerful my tongue was...I had spoken things into my marriage without realizing the power of life and death is in the words you say. The wrong interpretation can get you into trouble. We speak words from our mouths on situations that we see with our eyes or from the heart of others. We let other family members come into our marriage when we are having an argument with our spouse just to have someone on your side instead of taking it to the Lord

Proverbs 29:11 "A fool gives full vent to his anger, but a wise man keeps himself under control." I needed to know what matters from the heart, and what does the Lord love. I learned that it does not matter who is right or wrong but we can agree to disagree.

We have to cover each other in love. Not always feel like I won that battle this time. I learned the real name for marriage, **WORK**. Yes it takes working at your marriage; coming together as a unit and believing in each other, putting the Lord first. Marriage is ordained from God. God is the head, then man, then the woman, then the children. All these parts make up a family and in this order. When you are out of order, then there is a crack in the foundation. We have to find our place and seal up the crack. Give to our spouse the grace that you would want from him and that you want the Lord to give you. What does the Lord require of you? "To act justly and to love mercy and to walk humbly with your God."(Micah 6:8)

Chapter Ten

Man was not "created for woman, but woman for man"

Malachi 2:16 "Guard yourself in your spirit, and don't break faith." God created lines of authority in order for His created world to function smoothly. I read this statement and realized how true it was. We were created for God and He created men and women with unique and complementary characteristics. Have you ever heard the phrase "opposites attract"?

I believe, yes they do, because my husband and I are alike in some ways and different in other ways. A marriage needs the different ways in order to flow like water. No bondages! Just the flow of love and respect for each other. I learned I don't have to wait until I am 30 or 45 years into my marriage to see this happen, I can have it right now, so can you!

Chapter Eleven

Husbands love Your Wives

———————◆———✦———◆———————

<u>Ephesians 5:25-30</u>. "In this same way, husbands ought to love their wives as their own bodies. He who loves his wife loves himself. After all, no one hated his own body."

The wife must respect her husband; when you love yourself there is nothing that you wouldn't do for someone else. When I started dating my husband, I remember the first gifts I bought for him and how proud I was when he looked good in those hats. I remember going out of my way just to see the sensational smile of pleasure on his face when he received the hats. Marriage is like that, we have to sometimes go out of our comfort zone just to please our mate or see that face of pleasure. Get back into the habit of noticing one another with kindness and love. Do something special today for your Loved one, your Boo, your Boaz, Your Queen, your Duchess, Your Lady.

Chapter Twelve
Prayer of Love

Let me ask you, Are you prayerfully praying for your spouse? Are you showing the love of God in your marriage? Here is a prayer I believe will help you in praying for your spouse. Treat your husband or wife with respect and honor as God will have you do. Repeat after me.

Lord, help us to remember when we first met and the strong love that grew between us.

Teach us how to work that love into practical things so nothing can divide us.

We ask for words both kind and loving, and for hearts always ready to ask forgiveness as well as to forgive.

Dear Lord, we give full control of our marriage into Your hands, in Jesus' name Amen.

Proverbs 18:22 "a man's greatest treasure is his wife. She is a **gift** from the Lord." The heart of a family is the Lord. The core is love. The foundation is respect and honor. The reason is not the end but a **new beginning!**

Printed in the United States
By Bookmasters